SYMPHONY

D major/D-Dur/Ré majeur
K 202

Edited by/Herausgegeben von
Stanley Sadie

T0081309

Ernst Eulenburg Ltd

London · Mainz · Madrid · New York · Paris · Tokyo · Toronto · Zürich

Mozart, Symphony in D, K.202

Mozart's Symphony in D, K.202 [186b], known as No. 30, was composed in 1774, the last of the group of symphonies (including K.183 in G minor and K.201 in A) that Mozart wrote following his Viennese visit of 1773 in the course of which he had become acquainted with recent Viennese symphonic music. The symphony, though more direct and Italianate than certain others of this group, is closely related in the style of its thematic matter and its treatment of development to the Austrian divertimento tradition.

Mozart's autograph manuscript, in a Viennese private collection, is the principal source used in the preparation of this edition (there are no contemporary printed sources, the earliest edition dating from 1799). Photographic copies were kindly supplied by the Photogramm-Archiv of the National Bibliothek, Vienna. The manuscript is headed "Sinfonia" and, in the top right-hand corner of the first page, bears, in Mozart's hand, "di Wolfgango Amadeo Mozart a Salisburgo li 5 maggio 1774" (all but the signature are crossed out in a later hand).

Editorial additions (or very occasionally alterations, for consistency's sake) to phrasing, accidentals, dynamics etc. are distinguished by the use of a lighter or small type; *p*, etc., replace the original *pia:*, etc. An attempt has been made to observe Mozart's own distinction between staccato dots and dashes and to follow it through. Mozart's way of writing appoggiaturas has been altered to conform with modern methods, and slurs added. Mozart originally labelled the trumpet part "Trombe lunghe". For the sake of clarity, most of the abbreviated passages in the autograph are printed in full.

Stanley Sadie

Mozarts Symphonie in D, K.202, bekannt als No. 30, wurde 1774 komponiert und ist die letzte der Gruppe von Symphonien (zu der auch K.183 in G m und K.201 in A gehören) die er nach seinem Besuch in Wien schrieb; er war dort mit der neuesten Wiener symphonischen Musik bekannt geworden. Diese Symphonie, obgleich mehr von Italien beeinflusst, als gewisse andere dieser Gruppe, verrät doch im thematischen Stoff und in der Behandlung der Durchführung die Tradition des österreichischen Divertimentos.

Mozarts Autograph, in Wiener Privatbesitz, ist die Hauptquelle, die für diese Ausgabe benutzt wurde (es gibt keine gedruckte Ausgabe aus Mozarts Zeit; die erste datiert von 1799). Eine Photokopie wurde freundlicherweise vom Photogramm-Archiv der Österreichischen National-Bibliothek in Wien zur Verfügung gestellt. Das MS. ist überschrieben "Sinfonia" und oben rechts, von Mozarts Hand, bezeichnet "di Wolfgango Amadeo Mozart a Salisburgo li 5 maggio 1774" (alles ausser der Unterschrift von späterer Hand ausgestrichen).

Zusätze des Herausgebers (oder gelegentliche, durch die Konsequenz bedingte Korrekturen) in Bezug auf Phrasierung, Vorzeichen und Vortragsbezeichnungen sind durch dünneren oder kleineren Druck unterschieden; *pia* durch *p* ersetzt usw. Es wurde versucht, Mozarts eigene Unterscheidung zwischen staccato-Punkten und Keilen durchzuführen. Mozarts Notierung für Verzierungen wurde der modernen Schreibweise angepasst und Bögen hinzugefügt. Die Trompeten wurden von Mozart ursprünglich als "Trombe lunghe" notiert. Im Interesse der Klarheit sind die meisten der abgekürzten Schreibungen des Autographs voll gedruckt.

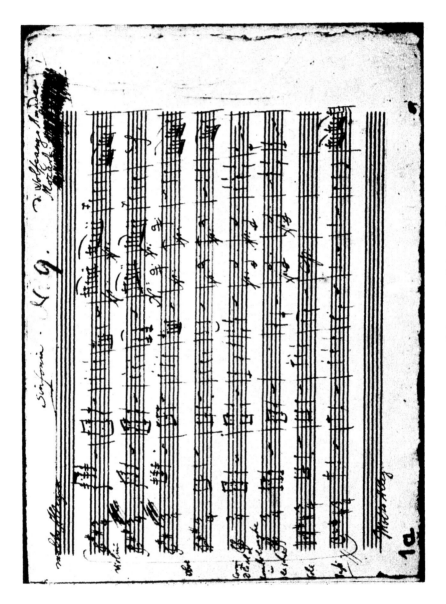

First page of the autograph (see preface)

SYMPHONY

I

W. A. MOZART
1756-1791
K.-V. 202

Molto allegro

2

4

6

E. E. 6452

12

14

E. E. 6452

II

Andantino con moto

III

Minuetto

20

Trio

41

Vl.

Vla.

Vcl.e
Cb.

47

Vl.

Vla.

Vcl.e
Cb.

54

Vl.

Vla.

Vcl.e
Cb.

[D.C. Minuetto]
p. 19

IV

24

26

30

E. E. 6452

32